IN THE STREET

Paul Noble

HODDER AND STOUGHTON
LONDON SYDNEY AUCKLAND TORONTO

MW01518333

To Nell Hacking, for memories.

Note to the reader

The words in heavy italics are explained in the glossary on page 32.

The Author's and Publishers' thanks are due to the following for permission to reproduce photographs:

t = top; b = bottom;
r = right; l = left

The Automobile Association: 14t; BBC Hulton Picture Library: 9t, 9b, 12, 16, 24, 27, 28; Barnaby's Picture Library: 7r, 11b; Camera Press: 8; City of Birmingham, Public Library: 7l; Chris Fairclough Colour Library: 3t, 25, 29b; Kirklees Metropolitan Council: 10; Mary Evans Picture Library: 11t, 22; Paul Noble: 6, 14b, 17t, 20l, 20r, 21t, 29l, 30, 31t; Peterborough Development Corporation: 31b; Popperfoto: 13r; Peter Sanders: 15; Peter Sheldon: 18, 19; Ian G. McM. Stewart: 23b; Telecom Technology Showcase: 23r; Telefocus; A British Telecom photograph: 19t; Tony Stone Photolibrary, London: 26; The Director, Wiltshire County Council, Library and Museum Service: 17b; Zefa: cover

Artists: Ann Baum; Tony Morris

British Library Cataloguing in Publication Data

Noble, Paul
  In the street.
  1. Great Britain. Towns. Streets, 1900-1987
  I. Title   II. Series
  941'.009'732

  ISBN 0-340-43127-X

Published by Hodder and Stoughton Children's Books, a division of Hodder and Stoughton Ltd, Mill Road, Dunton Green, Sevenoaks, Kent TN13 2YJ

Photoset by Litho Link Ltd, Welshpool, Powys, Wales

Printed in Belgium by Proost International Book Production

Designed by Sally Boothroyd

CONTENTS

THE STREET

1900 ➤ **1920** ➤ **1940** ➤

Squashed hedgehogs were not a common sight in 1900. Today they can be seen even on town streets. You do not have to be a super detective to work out why this should be. Streets have changed. But no two streets are ever exactly the same or entirely different. Places are different, just as times are different. Although today can be very different from yesterday, some things are the same.

As you travel down the street in the time line, you also travel through time. Of course the artist has cheated a little, but streets are a bit like this. Buildings and objects from different periods in history stand side by side. When you next look around your street, look carefully, for you will also be looking back in time.

1960

1980

My grandad was a young man when Queen Victoria died (1901), and for many years he sold newspapers on a street corner. I expect that you have already spotted the newspaper seller in the picture. If he could walk up this street now, what do you think would catch his eye?

You could try making a time line like this by collecting pictures from old magazines, or drawing them yourself. Add pictures at any time. This book will give you some ideas.

CLUES TO THE PAST

Half way up the wall of a house I know is a canal. I took the photograph below in case you did not believe me. Nearby is a large roundabout, and the noise of squeaking brakes and screeching tyres fills the air. At the turn of the century, walkers crossed the gently moving waters of a canal at this same spot. We know because we have old photographs and the memories of elderly people. Now we also have this enormous painting. Parts of the canal still exist, as do names like Canal Street and Canal Walk. Most streets contain clues to their past, but they are not always so easy to see.

PHOTOGRAPHS

Looking at photographs is one way we can discover differences between past and present. In both of the photographs opposite you can see the Church of St Martin-in-the-Fields. Some other features have remained too. Crossing the road in 1902 looks easy. Do you think that streets are better today than in the past? People assume that horses make less noise and less mess than cars. Would you agree, after looking at the evidence in the photograph?

A good way of finding out what it was really like in the recent past is to talk to an elderly person. Even your parents may have interesting childhood memories.

This mural shows what people would have seen here 50 years ago. ▼

Trafalgar Square in 1902. Compare it to the picture opposite and spot what has changed. ▼

Trafalgar Square today. What has remained the same in these two pictures? ▼

MEMORIES

Nell Hacking is retired now and lives alone. She talked to me about her childhood in London.

*When I was very small, about three, my dad worked for Pickfords. He had two horses, and one day he took me out on his cart. The road was cobbled and one of the horses slipped and fell over. I cried and cried! They took me into a café and gave me tea and a big slice of bread and **dripping**. The mug was huge. I couldn't hold it . . .*

*I remember the **lamplighter** with his long pole. Every evening he came round to light the gas lamps. He wore a long overcoat and a trilby hat. He must have walked for miles . . .*

We sat on the kerb and played 'Ollie Gobs', with stones. Is it called Five Stones? We played for hours on the kerb. You were quite safe. Not today though . . .

*My George was away at the war when the **doodlebugs** came over. I went to Bedfordshire for a few weeks. When I got back, a bomb had fallen in our street. All my windows had gone and everything was covered with glass. We had a good laugh, but I never went away again.*

PEOPLE

Between 1930 and 1975 the population of the world doubled. Britain's population increased from 38 million (1901) to over 51 million (1985). There are more people today but are they any different from previous *generations*? I wonder what our newspaper-seller would notice about the people in today's street. He would certainly see cleaner, healthier faces. We are more healthy, and indeed, more wealthy today. We also expect to live a lot longer.

IMMIGRANTS AND REFUGEES

There has always been a mixture of people in Britain. During the twentieth century, many new people came, including *refugees* from Russia, Poland, Hungary and Uganda. After the second world war, *immigrants* from the West Indies and India came seeking work and new homes. Many were encouraged to come to take jobs in companies like London Transport. A peak year was 1955 when 18,561 Jamaicans came to Britain. Most settled here. There are now 3 million coloured Britons.

Brixton was one of the places where the first immigrants settled in the 1950s. The market there is a lively colourful place.

WOMEN

During the two world wars this century, women had to do work usually carried

◀ Brixton market. Can you identify what is being sold on this stall?

A London street during the second world war. How many GIs can you count? ▶

out by men. They drove buses, mended roads and worked on farms. When the men returned from the wars, women were forced to give up these jobs. It was thought important that soldiers, sailors and airmen found work as quickly as possible. Because of recent laws, women can now do almost any job. Equal pay for equal work came in 1970. In 1975 it became illegal to choose people for a job just because of their sex. Can you think of any reasons why a job should be suitable solely for women or solely for men? Nowadays there are policewomen, female lorry drivers, and even a few firewomen. Many working women can be seen in a busy High Street. This change is a permanent one.

THE GI IN BRITAIN

Sometimes change is only temporary. For example, during the second world war there were hundreds of thousands of American servicemen (GIs) in Britain.

During which war was this photograph taken? What do you think is happening? ▼

They were a common sight in the streets. Indeed, 80,000 British girls married GIs. Now most of the GIs have gone. A few American airbases remain, but most of the Americans you meet in the street, are tourists. Some elderly Americans come to Britain each year to see where they were stationed during the war.

STREET TRADESMEN

A street trader in Piccadilly tried to sell me hot chestnuts on Boxing Day. At any time, on any street, there always seems to be someone ready to sell something. Double-glazing salesmen did not knock on doors in 1900 (double glazing was unheard of), but there were still many street tradesmen. Almost anything could be bought from a man with a cart. Hot pies and peas, chestnuts, baked potatoes, were all sold from carts which carried a fire to keep the food hot.

The milkman came round with a cart loaded with large churns of milk. Wearing a striped apron, he would ladle out *gills* of milk into jugs which people brought to his cart. He also sold skimmed milk, which was cheaper as it was thought only to be fit for cooking. Milk was later delivered to the doorstep in bottles. Since the second world war, these bottles have changed in shape and the glass has got thinner. Bottle technology has improved. Plastic cartons are also used. But doorstep deliveries are not always as frequent as they were, and one day they may disappear altogether.

Perhaps the most entertaining street salesman was the ironmonger. His covered cart was noisy and bright with pots, pans, kettles and bowls. Tradesmen were often very colourful characters, full of cheerful chatter for their customers. The carts were colourful, too. The streets were not really black and white – only the photographs were!

Milk was sold like this although this photograph is posed. How can you tell? ▼

◀ This cart must have rattled down the street. Do you have any pans like these in your kitchen?

Carnaby Street, in London, became world famous in the 1960s. The shops sold exciting clothes and everyone went to see, or to be seen. ▼

MEMORIES

A poor man from a lodging house used to come down our street carrying a sack on his back. He sold nettles for nettle broth. The children were frightened of him and used to run away . . .

In the evening you would hear cries of 'Cat's meat!' The cat's meat man carried slices of horsemeat on a wooden stick. Cats didn't eat from tins in those days.

CLOTHES AND FASHION

Clothing, hairstyles and fashions in women's make-up have changed frequently. We would need another book to show them all. You can sometimes date a picture by hairstyles alone.

I used to cut off the top of a stocking, and then roll it up until I had a circle. The circles sat on my head, then I would tuck all of my hair into it. I hardly ever went to the hairdresser's. This was in the 1940s.

When do you think the picture above was taken? The miniskirts tell us that it was during the 1960s. Are there any other clues? This kind of problem is one historians often have to deal with, asking not only how old something is, but how can you tell?

BUILDINGS

Most of the buildings in the street below are homes. Rows and rows of homes like these were built during the last century. They rarely had adequate heating and quickly became damp. Yet even though they lacked bathrooms, and the lavatory was often at the bottom of the garden, the houses were generally well cared for.

You always kept your doorstep clean and you whitened it with a scouring stone. The man who sold them carried a large enamel bowl on his head full of white and yellow stones.

Women and children have come to their clean white doorsteps to watch the electric cables being erected for the new trams. ▼

SLUM CLEARANCE

When the first world war ended, everyone wanted to get rid of bad houses and to build homes 'fit for heroes'. So, large numbers of new houses were built. The suburbs around big cities grew and grew. Some new towns, like Welwyn Garden City (1920), were started. Then came the second world war. Over 450,000 houses were destroyed by bombs. As soon as this war was over, work had to begin again. Bomb-damaged houses were replaced, and so were *slums*.

Rich and poor people lived and worked side by side during the war, and many of the well-off began to understand, for the first time, what poverty was like. All sorts of things shocked them. For example, many poor children had only one set of underwear for the winter. The government realised it had to do something. A start was made with housing. Thirty-two new towns were planned. People from overcrowded and war-damaged cities like Liverpool and London, moved into them. Old terraced

In Milton Keynes everything is new, even the names of the cycleways. This is known as a 'redway' and is called V8 because it runs vertically (V) on the town plan.

The collapse of these flats at Ronan Point in 1968 made many local authorities check carefully the state of their modern buildings. ▼

streets were flattened and slums were cleared. Between 1960 and 1964, 303,621 old houses were demolished and nearly a million people moved.

Would you rather live in the old street or the new? I expect that you can see the advantages of the new towns, but many people who actually moved to them wished that they could go back to their old homes.

CONCRETE AND HIGH-RISE
One way of building lots of homes very quickly, especially if space is limited, is to build upwards. So, using concrete instead of brick and stone, high-rise flats were erected. These homes were not suitable for everybody. Concrete could be cold and damp. Some people felt lonely. Flats did not make streets, but stood in blocks and squares like a child's building bricks.

In the 1960s, when there was a rush to build, many mistakes were made. In 1968, a gas explosion started the disastrous collapse of the concrete flats at Ronan Point, London. The concrete mix was faulty.

Recently there has been a return to building houses rather than flats, and more use is now made of brick. Britain is still short of good quality homes, but homes are getting better. In 1971 one in three homes had some form of central heating. By 1985, it was two out of three. Four million people owned their own homes in 1951. In 1985 the number was 14 million.

NEW BUILDINGS
One building new to this century is the car park. Car parks were not needed until there were too many cars to park in the street. Now cars are stacked above and below street level.

Garages are also new. The first petrol station opened in Aldermaston, Berkshire in 1920. Until then petrol was sold by ironmongers and even some hotels. Many garages opened in the 1930s when motoring became popular.

NEW DESIGNS
With a little bit of practice, it is possible to estimate the age of buildings. High-rise concrete is almost certainly 1960s. *Bay-windowed* houses in long suburban roads are probably 1920s or 1930s. When do you think the building opposite was erected?

▲ One of the very first AA petrol stations in Hampshire. Can you imagine how it would cope with modern traffic?

Friday prayer in Norwich. Christians once worshipped in this chapel; now Moslems do the same. ▶

You can't see in, but can they see out? A modern glass building in Swindon. ▼

Modern technology and materials make this kind of design possible. Glass is used as a mirror. During the daytime the building seems bare, almost sinister. At night, though, when the lights are on, it comes alive and can look very beautiful. Buildings have faces, like people. This is a 1980s face. Collecting faces, by taking photographs or making sketches, can be fun. It can also help you to work out the age of a building.

NEW USES

But faces can lie. Is this a church below? Originally, yes. Now it is a mosque. It has changed in use since it was built. This has happened to many buildings.

Cinemas have become bingo halls, old stations have become car parks, and churches have become warehouses. Fewer Christians now attend Church, so many churches and chapels stand empty. However, the numbers of Muslims, Sikhs and Hindus are increasing. The unused buildings can be ideal for the celebration of their faiths.

Tracing changes in building use can reveal much of a street's history. Local reference libraries have old maps, plans and photographs that will help you to do this.

SHOPS

At the beginning of the century, a shopworker's life was very hard. A law, passed in 1912, insisted that shopworkers were given a half-day holiday each week. Until then, they only had Sundays off. Shop owners often lived above their shops. This is far from common today. Many of these flats are now empty or neglected. Look at the windows above your High Street shops and you will see what I mean.

Shops have changed more than any other buildings in the street. And yet it is easy to find shops that have hardly changed in a hundred years.

The photograph opposite was taken in 1987, but it could just as easily have been taken 80 years ago – except for one fact, electricity. Compare the next picture with the last. They were taken eighty-four years apart. Not everything changes.

Walking down a High Street in 1945 or even 1950, you would find shops little

Most shops are to be found in a street called a High Street, although this may not be the street's proper name. Nell Hacking remembers the High Street near her childhood home.

There were no supermarkets. In the shops you joined the queue. You said what you wanted and they served you. I think supermarkets make you spend more.

Queuing was unavoidable when shops were small. Personal service also took time. During the second world war, there were particularly long queues because many things were *rationed*.

◀ Early in the war these smart ladies had no difficulty shopping. Bananas are on sale, yet these later disappeared from the shops. Why?

Before mass advertising, shop windows, like the ones above, were used to promote as many goods as possible. ▶

changed since the turn of the century. Until 1950, most shops were still small single units. Ninety per cent of all shops were like this in the 1930s, although shops with many branches (chain stores), were growing. Chain stores like Boots and Sainsburys have survived; others, like Macfisheries, have gone. Small corner shops first began to disappear with slum clearance. They were rarely rebuilt. Then in 1950, the first supermarkets opened. Small shops soon found that they could not compete in choice or price. They started to go out of business. Try making a survey of the shopping habits of people in your area. How many of them, I wonder, use corner shops for most of their shopping?

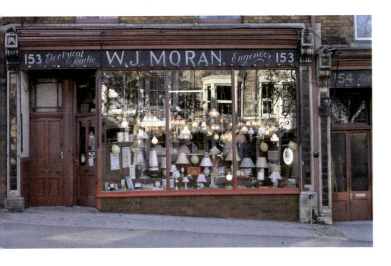

▲ Most lights are sold in big department stores today, but some small shops like this one can still be found.

Our corner shop was very handy. On Monday morning mum sent us to the shop with an empty cup and three-halfpence (less than half a modern penny). We bought pickle to eat with Sunday's leftovers. Monday was washday and mum couldn't stop to make a meal.

Supermarkets and *hypermarkets* are very handy too, if you have a car. The largest ones do not fit in the High Street and are built on the outskirts of towns.

DISPLAYING THE GOODS

Shops have displayed their goods outside or under *awnings* for hundreds of years. Very few food shops do this now, because traffic fumes and dirt spoil the food. Until recently, many butchers used to hang up their meat on rails outside.

In the picture below notice how even in this very busy street, everyone has time to stop and stare at the camera.
A cameraman was not a common sight in 1913. Have you noticed the advertisements? The amount of advertising increased rapidly after the first world war. Quaker Oats, Kelloggs and Ovaltine quickly became household names. Advertisements are now everywhere, and some shops paste them on their windows. The first television advertising began in 1955. Shops try to make special displays of items advertised on television.

NEW SHOPS

Have you ever heard of the Spencer Mark One Junior? It was the first dry-cleaning machine small enough to fit into a High Street shop. It was introduced in 1949. Dry cleaning shops, and of course launderettes, are now found in every High Street. Charity shops like Oxfam and Sue Ryder are also new to the High Street. Unisex hair salons do not go back more than about fifteen years. Not long ago, men and boys went to the barber's for a hair cut. There was only one style – short back and sides!

New types of shops have sprung up because of new inventions, such as radios, televisions, videos and computers.

The picture opposite shows one of the newest High Street shops with a very modern front. It has a simple uncluttered

◀ Hats are in fashion in this crowded street. Can you see what is being sold by Briggs and Company?

Cromwell St. Swindon. 465

You can almost smell this picture. The noise, the dirt and the smells would be quite different from today, but not necessarily worse. What do you think? ▶

display, lots of colour, and big plate glass windows. Push-button telephones are part of the new technology. Many recent changes in shops and shopping have been due to the revolution in electronics. Cash dispensers, credit cards and electronic theft controls are all part of it. But some changes have had little to do with technology. The increase in health food shops is one example. You may be able to think of others.

MARKET DAY

Below you can see market day in a High Street eighty years ago. There are no high-tech shop fronts or electronic devices to be seen here. Horses are tied up outside a pub down the street, just like in a cowboy film. Have you noticed what the shop nearest the camera is selling? Look carefully. There is a lot going on. This market was closed in 1939 because of health regulations. But all kinds of markets still survive. Not everyone wants to shop in supermarkets. Not everyone can afford to.

◀ These shops are recent additions to the High Street. Perhaps there is one near where you live.

ADVERTISEMENTS, SIGNS AND SYMBOLS

This bicycle should not be here. Do you know why? ▶

What kind of school sign do you have near your school? If you designed a new one what would you change? ▼

Advertising has had to be controlled by law. You cannot advertise just where you like. An advertisement may not tell a direct lie. Possibly the most famous advertisements in any British street are the illuminated ones in Piccadilly Circus, London.

▲ This sign is so bright, it is hardly possible to miss it. It cost thousands of pounds to make and erect.

The brightly coloured modern sign (left) is an advertisement, but it also gives directions. Which way to the AA? It is interesting to see the AA on this sign because in 1908 the AA put up the very first road signs for motorists. As the speed of traffic increased, roadside signs got bigger. Motorway signs are biggest of all. Which is bigger, your house or a signpost at a motorway junction? When the 30 mph speed limit was introduced in all built-up areas (1935), the familiar limit sign appeared. Symbols, such as the circle and the triangle, are much used on road signs.

The circular traffic sign is a recent one. Even before Britain entered the Common Market (1973), experts thought that Europe needed standard traffic signs. So British traffic signs were changed to fit into the European system. 'Halt! Major Road Ahead' signs were replaced by 'Give Way'. The latest signs are in the Highway Code. Some old signs can still be found in streets where nobody has yet bothered to remove them. Look at the school sign in the last picture. The reflectors in the triangle seem to have disappeared, but otherwise it is intact. Here is a bit of the past in the present. When this sign was erected, school uniform was common, and satchels and caps were in fashion. The boy is marching smartly to school with a book in his hand, ignoring the girl. What do modern school signs show?

Some street signs are actually on the surface of the street – yellow lines for example. Look at the picture above. This delivery bicycle was made at a time when yellow lines had not been invented. Perhaps it has been parked for a long time! White lines were first painted down the middle of the road as an experiment in 1924. Yellow lines now snake their way along almost every kerbside.

Thousands of advertisements, pub signs, shop signs, symbols and *logos* decorate the High Street. If you started to count them in your street, you would probably be surprised to find how many there are.

STREET FURNITURE

HORSES

In the early years of this century, traffic not only needed controlling – it needed to be given a drink as well! Horses kept the wheels turning. The Metropolitan Drinking Fountain and Cattle Trough Association provided over 1000 granite drinking troughs to refresh horses particularly on hills. These can still be found, especially in the London area. They are sometimes used as flower boxes. Even in 1952, there were 300,000 horses working on farms. By 1979 there were only 3575 left.

ELECTRICITY

Electricity was used in the street even before it was supplied to most homes. Overhead cables were erected to carry electricity to power electric trams in 1902. Trams finished working in London in 1952 but continued in Glasgow until 1962. The poles that used to carry the electric cables can sometimes be seen supporting modern street lighting.

Letter-boxes, lamp-posts, *bollards*, traffic lights, and other fixed objects found in streets, are called street furniture. Most street furniture is to do with traffic.

Traffic lights were used by the police in Piccadilly (1925), because traffic needed controlling. Electrically operated lights were first tried out in Wolverhampton (1926). Look closely at the traffic lights near you. Some old ones have STOP written on the red light.

Parking meters were introduced in London in 1958.

◀ This horse looks more interested in the pub than in the water trough! The trough is conveniently placed for the driver rather than for the horse.

One of the last trams in Glasgow. Can you guess why they were replaced? ▶

The tracks on which the trams used to run were generally pulled up or buried beneath new tarmac.

Lamp-standards are perhaps the most beautiful items of street furniture. Modern ones can be slim and elegant. Old cast iron gas standards, now fitted with electric lights, are very ornate. In Trafalgar Square there are some magnificent ones (see page 7).

The police introduced a new piece of furniture in 1988 when the first crime-watching video cameras were fixed above special pavement trouble spots. These might become very common. But the Metropolitan Police telephone box (Dr Who's Time Machine, or 'Tardis'), is now quite rare. The last one was withdrawn from use in 1969. There is such a wide variety of street furniture, that 'furniture spotting' is a growing hobby. Some people even collect the furniture itself. That is why old train signals and lamp standards can appear unexpectedly in front gardens.

TELEPHONE BOXES

Tracking down different telephone boxes can be fun. There are a surprising number of different designs. Design number 1 dates from 1921. Many of these old telephone boxes are protected as historic buildings.

▲ This is one of the first telephone kiosks. How many differently designed kiosks can you spot in your area?

TRAFFIC

be heard in today's street, including electronic ones. A modern street is very noisy. Stricter controls on vehicle noise were introduced in 1988.

Eleanor Hopkinson, from Heckmondwike, Yorkshire, was brought up with horses. Her father ran a transport business. She remembers the horses being dressed up for the *Whitsuntide* parade.

My dad spent hours grooming and trimming before the parade. He sat up all night with the horses to make sure that they didn't lie down and mess themselves up.

Most traffic was horse-powered at the turn of the century. Even engine power was first measured in 'horse power'. Can you imagine what these busy horse-filled streets must have smelt or sounded like? Many different sounds can

5164. REGENT STREET.

The increase from 18,000 motor vehicles in 1904 to 19 million in 1985, has made a great deal of difference to streets. Even the surface has changed. Bumpy stone *setts* have been replaced by smoother surfaces more suited to fast vehicles. Anyone could drive a motor car until 1934 when driving tests were introduced. Some elderly drivers have never had to take a test.

ACCIDENTS AND CRIME
The first person to be killed in a motor accident died in August 1896. In 1985, 5200 people died and 71,000 were seriously injured on the roads. The worst year was 1941 when deaths totalled 9444. Streets were extremely dangerous during the war because of the blackout. Alcohol is today's greatest danger. Over half of all crimes are traffic crimes. In 1970, nearly one million people were found guilty of traffic crimes, compared to only 2548 in 1900.

CARS AND BIKES
Since 1960, public transport has been used less and less. Most families now own cars. Some new vehicles, such as electric cars and computer controlled buses, have appeared. Old inventions such as trolley buses and trams, have now gone. Since 1980, the bicycle has become more popular again, just as it was in Edwardian times. Bicycles sales are up, and new bike lanes and cyclepaths have been created.

Simple answers, such as making streets one-way, can solve traffic problems. Sometimes by-passes or fly-overs have to be built. You probably have traffic problems near you. Have you any ideas on how they might be solved?

◄ Different carriages were designed for different purposes. Can you identify the taxis, buses and lorries in Regent Street at the turn of the century?

Traffic jams outside Harrods, the famous department store, are a common sight. ▶

LEISURE AND PLEASURE

TELEVISION, MUSIC HALLS AND CINEMAS

In 1945 there were very few television sets. Many were bought in 1953 for the Coronation of Queen Elizabeth II. Between 1950 and 1955 the number of television sets increased a massive ten times. Watching television is now the most common leisure activity.

Music halls were very popular at the turn of the century. They were lively places, where noisy audiences liked to join in the songs. However, when 'moving pictures' arrived, music halls were finished. By 1914 there were already 3500 'picture houses' in Great Britain. At first the pictures were in black and white and silent. A pianist accompanied the action. He also filled-in when the projector broke down. When the 'talkies' came, most people went to the cinema at least once a week. By 1939 there were nearly 5000 cinemas.

Today, television has destroyed most of them. Television means you do not have to go to the pictures, the pictures come to you. Some cinemas have been turned into modern multi-screen theatres. Many have simply been demolished.

Eighty years ago, not even the world's cleverest person could have solved this riddle. I expect that you have.

▼ The answer to the riddle is in here.

STREET GAMES AND SPORT

Before television, children played more street games. When I was a boy, I played Tip-Cat, Knocking-Down-Ginger and my favourite, Hot Rice. Do you know them? Your parents and grandparents can probably tell you about the games they played.

Sport is played by more people than ever before, but fewer go out to watch it. Football had twice as many spectators in 1950 than it has today. Millions of pounds have been spent on sports halls. There is probably one near you. Indoor sports like table-tennis (10,000 players in 1930, but 200,000 in 1967), have grown rapidly.

◀ Going to the cinema was a regular event before the days of television.

You can tell by the clothes, and sometimes by the games, when these games were played. ▼

GAMBLING

Gambling has always been a popular pastime, especially amongst men. Before betting shops were allowed by law (1960), men called 'bookies' took bets on street corners. They had 'runners' to watch out for the police. The number of betting shops and bingo halls has fallen recently, but there is now much more gambling on fruit machines.

HOLIDAYS

As recently as 1947, half the population had no annual holidays at all. Hardly anyone went abroad. Families from all over Britain now fly to find sunshine. Spain is the most popular destination. You do not have to travel far down the High Street to find a travel agent. In the 1930s a travel agent would have booked your transport and hotel individually. These are now sold as part of a complete package. Package holidays are cheaper.

Look at your family's holiday destinations on a map. Go back as far as you can. Include grandparents' holidays if possible.

EATING OUT

There have been some fairly dramatic changes in food shops, especially since the second world war. Greater use of refrigerators, microwave ovens and food preservatives, has led to more and more 'fast foods' being sold. We have copied some American eating habits. Although fish and chips are still sold, there are many other types of take-away foods. When your grandparents were young, they would not have had burgers, *kebabs* or chop suey to eat.

Can you see how many different countries are represented in the picture below? This is a small English country town. There is even more choice in a big city. Foreign food is now so common that one shop I know advertises that it sells 'English' fish and chips! Eating out is not just convenient, it is usually a pleasure as well. You may have been to a birthday party at a burger bar or a pizza house.

Restaurants, sports halls, saunas, cinemas, theatres and video shops, are just some of the places in a street to do with leisure. Are there any more? How many do you think there would have been eighty years ago?

In a number of towns, traditional street fairs that go back hundreds of years, block the roads on special days each year. Recently, street carnivals have been introduced by West Indians in places like Notting Hill. On very special occasions, such as the end of a war, street parties have replaced the traffic. Why is the street party below being held?

◀ If you check the area where you live, you will probably find food from all over the world being sold.

◀ Pie and eel shops used to be very common, particularly in London. They have largely been replaced by new food shops as eating habits have changed.

Be a detective. These children are celebrating a Royal event. Which one? Do you know of any other occasions when street parties were held? ▶

TODAY AND TOMORROW

In some ways the traditional High Street is being destroyed: big chain stores are replacing the smaller individual shops and huge out-of-town stores are taking people away from town centres. Also heavy traffic, which causes noise and fumes, has made shopping tiring and unpleasant in many streets. Vandals frequently spoil walls and buildings with aerosol paint cans.

However, attempts are continually being made to make the High Street more attractive and convenient. Sometimes this means preserving something of beauty already in the street. Important buildings are 'listed' as being of historic interest. This means that they can't be demolished, or even altered, without permission from the town council. Some listed buildings, like telephone box number one (page 23), were built this century.

Some towns, for example Oxford, have introduced 'Park and Ride' systems. This means that people can park their cars outside the town and catch special buses to the shops. The buses travel in bus lanes that are closed to cars. This reduces the number of cars in the town centre.

PRECINCTS

Another way to improve a High Street is to turn it into a precinct. This may mean roofing over the street, building car parks nearby (often underground ones), banning traffic and adding flowers, fountains, statues and music.

This sounds perfect, but many indoor shopping precincts have problems: they can be stuffy and badly lit and shoppers are constantly under the eye of security men. Music, designed to make you feel relaxed and spend more, is sometimes played constantly. Soft and unexciting, it is known as 'musak'.

HOMES

People nearly always take pride in the streets in which they live. Front gardens usually have special care lavished on them. In the early part of the century front gardens had fashionable and easily pruned privet, laurel or box hedges.

During the 1960s and 1970s it became popular to plant fast-growing conifers in order to get privacy. People did not realise how quickly they grew. Unpruned, they have grown to become green giants dominating small streets.

The most important street to you is, certainly, the street where you live. Did it exist in 1900? Perhaps, like a true historian, you can find out the history of your street. How can you find out? You can use old photographs, maps, newspapers, books, old family albums, elderly people, museums, libraries and, of course, your eyes.

◀This statue adds colour to Brunel shopping precinct.

Peterborough today is very different from earlier in the century. What advantages can you see in shopping in a place like this? ▶

◀ Small gardens are not made for big plants, but in recent years fast-growing conifers have been planted in many unsuitable places.

GLOSSARY AND INDEX

awning stretched canvas cover that comes out from a wall and provides protection from rain or sun

bay window window that juts out from the line of a building

bollards short posts used to keep traffic from a pathway

doodlebugs commonly used word for German flying bombs

dripping the melted fat from roasted meat. It used to be spread on bread like butter

generation group of people born about the same time. A new generation starts about every 30 years

gill quarter of a pint

hypermarket very large self-service store outside a town

immigrants foreigners who come into a country to settle

kebab vegetables and meat grilled together on a skewer

lamplighter man who lit street gas lamps using a long pole

logo design chosen as the mark of an organisation, like British Rail's crossing arrows

preservatives chemicals added to food to prevent them from perishing

rationed limited to small amounts

refugees people seeking shelter and safety in a foreign country because of some danger in their own

setts small stone paving blocks used to surface town streets

slums dirty and overcrowded part of a city lived in by poor people

Whitsuntide the week including the Christian festival of Whit Sunday which commemorates the time when the Holy Spirit came upon Jesus' disciples